The Railways of Exeter,
and Axminster to Lyme Regis
in photographs by J. C. Way
Neil Butters

Castle Class No. 7001 *Sir James Milne* brings a Down express into Exeter St. David's. September 1957.

No. 4082 *Windsor Castle* with an Up express at Cowley Bridge, early 1957.

© Neil Butters, 2016
First published in the United Kingdom, 2016,
by Stenlake Publishing Ltd.
www.stenlake.co.uk
ISBN 9781840337433

The publishers regret that they cannot supply
copies of any pictures featured in this book.

Printed by
Blissetts, Roslin Road, Acton, W3 8DH

No. 7031 *Cromwell's Castle* hauls the Up Royal Duchy past Exwick Fields, Exeter on 27th April 1957.

Foreword

Although our father grew up in Cornwall, his first job as an adult took him to Devon. He lived in Ashburton, then Axminster where he met our mother, Pam; then Braunton and Exeter. His interest in steam trains and photography gave him two hobbies that combined well. We as a family always travelled by train to see our grandparents in Lyme Regis and Penzance and he took every opportunity to photograph trains wherever we went. We remember him hopping on and off trains at stations along the way in order to do this, much to the consternation of our mother! He also spent time at weekends near the stations where we lived, often with us in tow, photographing as many different engines as he could. As we grew older we enjoyed being out and about with him and then working alongside him as he developed the rolls of film. We are pleased to see his efforts now reaching a wider audience.

Jan Walker, Anne Pickard and Susan Way

This book is dedicated to the memory of our mother, Pam, much loved wife of John Corin Way.

J. C. Way photographer.

No. 6814 *Enborne Grange* pulls into Exeter St. David's station in October 1955.

SR West Country Class 7P5F 4-6-2 No. 34001 *Exeter* draws into Exeter Central, October 1955.

West Country Class Pacific No. 34037 *Clovelly* arrives with a Down train at Exeter Central in October 1955. The two discs indicate a Waterloo – Plymouth train.

SR T9 'Greyhound' Class 2P 4-4-0 No. 30715 arriving at Exeter Central. Dugald Drummond design for the London & South Western Railway (LSWR). October 1955.

SR S15 Class 6F 4-6-0 no. 30827 heading a Down train east of Exeter Central, January 1956.

No. 7909 *Heveningham Hall* with an Up train at Cowley Bridge in 1956.

N Class 2-6-0 No. 31830 with a Down goods train on the SR line near Cowley Bridge, taken from a field adjoining the bridge near the Earl of Iddesleigh's estate. The headcode indicates a Meldon Quarry ballast train. 12th November 1956.

A splendid shot of a BR Standard loco hauling a short, two-coach passenger train through Cowley Bridge Junction off the Southern line, early 1957.

Class 2800 8F 2-8-0 No. 3834 with a Down goods crossing the River Exe between Cowley Bridge and Stoke Canon, 2nd February 1957.

1400 Class 1P 0-4-2 Tank No. 1405 with an Exeter – Dulverton train near Cowley Bridge, 2nd February 1957.

No. 1019 *County of Merioneth* leaves Exeter St. David's with an Up train in 1957.

No. 5096 *Bridgwater Castle* at Cowley Bridge. Note the Kitchen Car leading. 1957.

No. 5004 *Llanstephan Castle* with a westbound express out of Exeter St. David's on 18th May 1957.

May 1957. No. 4978 *Westwood Hall* pilots another GWR 4-6-0 on a Penzance – Manchester express at Cowley Bridge. Note the Travelling Post Office (TPO) vehicle.

2800 Class No. 2857 at Cowley Bridge on 13th July 1957.

No. 2857 at Cowley Bridge, 13th July 1957.

King Class 8P 4-6-0 No. 6009 *King Charles II* at Cowley Bridge. 13th July 1957.

Castle Class No. 5046 *Earl Cawdor* approaching Cowley Bridge with an Up Penzance – Swansea express, 13th July 1957.

Unrebuilt Battle of Britain No. 34060 *25 Squadron* at Cowley Bridge. Note the signal set for the Southern line. A WR locomotive waits with its train in the goods loop. 13th July 1957.

A 'King' brings a Down train into Exeter St. David's, 20th July 1957.

Castle Class No. 5052 *Earl of Radnor* with an Up Penzance – Paddington express arriving at Exeter St. David's. 1st September 1957.

Battle of Britain No. 34059 *Sir Archibald Sinclair* heads an Up train near Beacon Lane, Exeter (near Exmouth Junction). 15th September 1957. The locomotive is now preserved, at the Bluebell Railway.

Merchant Navy Class 8P 4-6-2 No. 35012 *United States Lines* heads the 12.00 pm Exeter – Waterloo express, half a mile from Exeter Central, 22nd September 1957.

West Country No. 34030 *Watersmeet* **with the 11.25 am Exeter – Kingswear at Exeter St. David's, 22nd October 1957.**

No. 6026 *King John* with the 11.23 am from Exeter St. David's (Penzance – Paddington train), 22nd October 1957.

No. 5023 *Brecon Castle* with the 9.30 am Paddington – Plymouth train leaving Exeter St. David's. 24th October 1957.

No. 6027 *King Richard I* (with double chimney) with the Mayflower at Exeter St. David's, 14th December 1957.

No. 6025 *King Henry III* passing Cowley Bridge with the 6.25 am Up from Penzance (11.23 from Exeter). Loco has double chimney and four-row Superheater, 11th January 1958.

No. 6004 *King George III* (fitted with double chimney and 4-row Superheater) heads the Down Cornish Riviera Express past Exwick Fields, Exeter, 2nd March 1958.

No. 5959 *Mawley Hall* with the 2.20 pm Exeter St. David's – Kingswear train. Note the impressive signals. 2nd March 1958.

No. 6002 *King William IV* heads the Up Mayflower passing Exwick Fields, Exeter, 8th March 1958.

4500 No. 5530 heads a Heathfield – Exeter branch train at Alphington Halt, near Exeter St. Thomas, 8th March 1958.

No. 6010 *King Charles I* with the Down Cornish Riviera Express passing Exeter St. Thomas, 30th March 1958.

No. 4948 *Northwick Hall* at Exeter St. Thomas, with the Down 2.25 pm, 30th March 1958.

No. 3440 *City of Truro* heads the 9.35 am Exeter – Penzance excursion past Exwick Fields, Exeter, 25th May 1958.

No. 6017 *King Edward IV* hauls the 11.23 am train from Exeter St. David's (Penzance – Paddington train) passing Cowley Bridge, 26th May 1958.

Axminster to Lyme Regis

A branch line train, conveying one coach only, crosses Cannington Viaduct at Uplyme on the Lyme Regis Branch. Lyme Regis itself is in Dorset, but almost all of the rest of the branch was in Devon. October 1951.

Adams design for the LSWR Class 0415 1P 4-4-2 Tank built 1885 No. 30584 passes Uplyme on the Lyme Regis Branch. The single disc at the bottom confirms an Axminster – Lyme Regis train. May 1956.

An Adams Tank comes off Cannington Viaduct at Uplyme, 21st April 1957.

0415 Class No. 30582 heads a Down train at Uplyme, 23rd April 1958. The small oval at the bottom of the smokebox door is the shed code; 72A was the code for Exmouth Junction plus sub-sheds, including Lyme Regis. Its sister locomotive No. 30583 has been preserved, on the Bluebell Railway in Sussex.

0415 Class No. 30584 with an Axminster – Lyme Regis train having just left Combpyne, 24th April 1959.

Class 0415 No. 30582 with an Axminster – Lyme Regis train passing Hook Farm, Uplyme, 13th April 1961.

S15 4-6-0 No. 30845 with an Up goods at Axminster sidings, 3.00 pm, 15th April 1961.

LMS Class 2 2-6-2 Tank No. 41292 arrives at Lyme Regis from Axminster, 28th April 1962.

41292 again, this time at Axminster: Lyme Regis Branch platform. This photo was taken by daughter Janet on 27th April 1963.